Skeletons

Have you ever seen
a skeleton?

This skeleton belongs to a creature that can slither and slide.

It is the skeleton of...

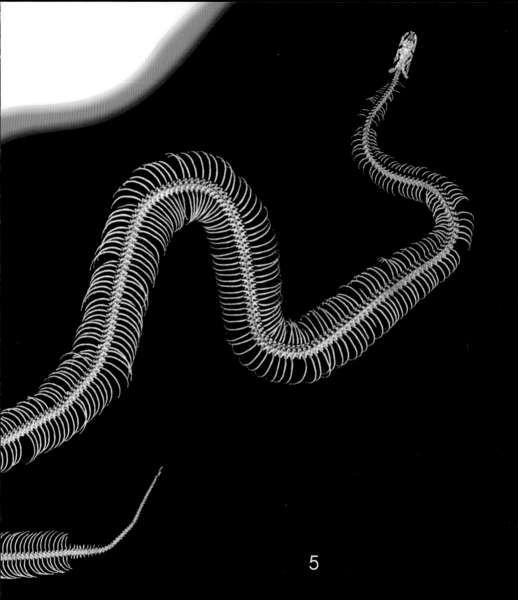

a snake.

A snake skeleton
is mostly backbone
and ribs.

This skeleton belongs to a creature that can dive and swim.

It is the skeleton of...

8

9

a fish.

A fish skull has
more than 100 bones.
A human skull has
about 28 bones.

This is the skeleton of a creature that can flap and fly.

It is the skeleton of...

13

a bird.

This bird is a swan.
Birds have bones that
are hollow and lightweight.
Light bones help them fly.

This skeleton belongs to a creature that can gallop and trot.

It is the skeleton of...

16

a horse.

A horse has long leg bones that help it run fast.

This skeleton belongs to a creature that can walk, run, and play.

It is the skeleton of...

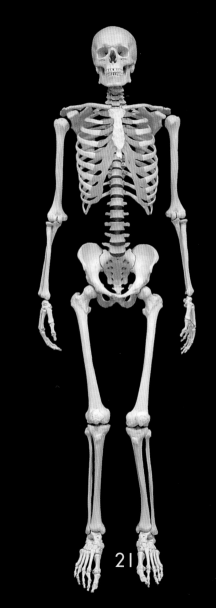

a person.

22

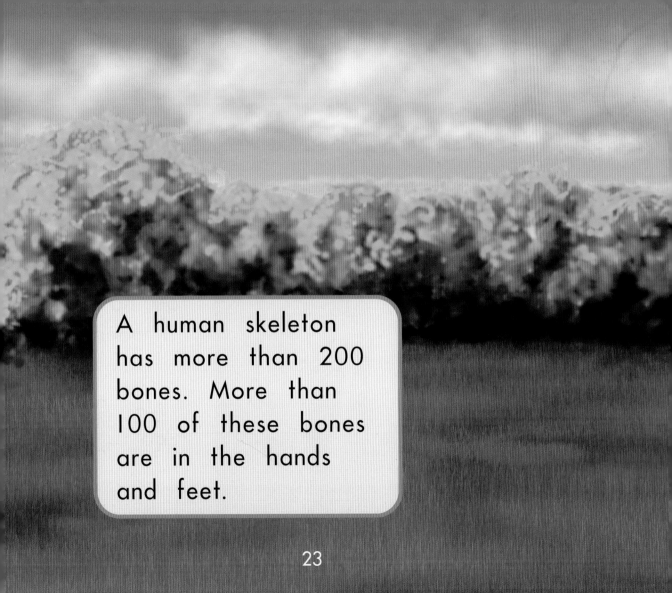

A human skeleton has more than 200 bones. More than 100 of these bones are in the hands and feet.

Your Skeleton

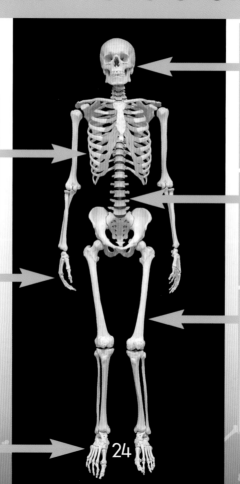

You have 12 pairs of ribs.

You have 27 bones in each hand.

You have 26 bones in each foot.

The smallest bones in your body are inside your ear.

You have 33 bones in your spine.

The longest bones in your body are your thigh bones.